£1.25

MILLOM CASTLE, BY S. BUCK, 1739.

: The :

Millom District

∞

A History

∞

FRANK WARRINER.

Republished by
Michael Moon at The Beckermet Bookshop, Cumberland
1974

First published 1932 © Frank Warriner
Republished by Michael Moon at
The Beckermet Bookshop, Beckermet
Cumberland

© Michael Moon 1974

Also by Frank Warriner:
Millom People and Places

ISBN 0 904131 05 X

Printed and bound in Great Britain by
The Scolar Press Ltd, Ilkley, Yorkshire

INTRODUCTION.

THIS book makes no claim to be a complete history of the old parish of Millom; it is an account of the antiquities of a small corner of Cumberland—the cloth upon which Celts, Vikings, monks and mighty medieval families wove the intricate pattern of their lives, the endless cycle of birth, toil, passion and death. They ruled, built, drained and planted it; few attained fame, but all filled a definite place in English history. This heritage is ours, their only memorial the woods they hunted, the circles and cairns they built, the monkish Latin charters they signed, their church and castle, and a sprinkling of names upon a map.

The main printed sources used are *The Register of St. Bees, The Furness Coucher Book,* and the two series of *Transactions of the Cumberland and Westmorland Antiquarian Society* (especially the articles, " Millom Castle and the Hudlestons " by Mr. H. S. Cowper, F.S.A., and " On the Identification of Some Ancient Places in South Cumberland " by the Rev. W. S. Sykes), *Lake District History* by Mr. W. G. Collingwood, F.S.A., Mr. Alfred Fell's *Early Iron Industry of Furness,* and Dr. Nightingale's *The Ejected Of 1662.*

My thanks are due to the Rev. W. S. Sykes for help in all branches of South Cumbrian history willingly given during the past ten years; to Rear-Admiral R. Hudleston, who has corrected and added to the history of his family; to the Rev. W. S. Sherwen; to Mr. C. H. Vance, of New York, who is engaged upon a life of Dr. Myles Cooper; to Miss Mary C. Fair; to Mr. J. Cooper; and, finally, to the Council of the Cumberland and Westmorland Antiquarian Society for the loan of the blocks for all illustrations in this booklet except that of the Duddon Furnace, which is reproduced from a photograph in the Barrow Public Library by the courtesy of the Librarian.

FRANK WARRINER.

CONTENTS.

———

———

Illustrations.

———

I.—TO THE CONQUEST.

THE Lordship of Millom consisted originally of the triangular plateau of moorland between the Esk and the Duddon. Its edges slope steeply owing to the influence of the Scafell glaciers which carved out their way down the valleys to meet the mass of Scotch ice flowing across the Solway from Dumfries and Galloway past Ravenglass and Millom, shearing off in its course the gentle slopes, thus forming the steep western escarpments of Black Combe. Gradually the warmth increased, the lobe of ice covering the north began to retreat, Whicham Valley, still blocked by ice, became a lake which found one outlet through Ghyll Scaur, and left on Black Combe traces of three lake shores.

After the retreat of the ice, during a period of dry warmth when the level of lakes and tarns was lower than to-day, men of the Neolithic or New Stone Age spread into the district. They were small, long-skulled Iberians, peaceful barrow and circle building men already fully developed in their own culture forms, who dwelt in small groups near the coast, on the uplands in hilly districts and occasionally by lakes and tarns, for the valleys and low-lying land were often waterlogged and filled with trees and scrub; the higher slopes were wooded, but the level shelves between mountain and valley offered a hard living without difficult drainage and clearing. Stone Age man buried his uncremated dead beneath long barrows in cists or chambers of stone. Their implements were of highly polished stone. Finds in the Millom district include a beautifully finished flint axe 13½ inches long, found near Lowscales in 1824 and now at Broadgate; 2 stone hammers and 2 celts in Whicham; 2 stone axes at Fenwick; part of a stone hammer at Kirksanton, another in Ulpha, and flint arrow heads at Scots' Croft, Millom Vicarage, and at Esp Hall, Ulpha. Some of these implements are of much later date, since stone continued in use during the Bronze Age.

The Stone Age passed with the coming of the bronze-using Goidels, a Keltic tribe, tall, fair-haired, with high cheek-bones and round heads, who arrived in Britain about B.C. 1800 and spread slowly northwards over our uplands. They had distinctive pottery and buried their dead, after cremation, in round barrows. Their homesteads were fenced about by walls and banks against wolves and other marauders. It was this people who left us the Barnscar " village " and the numerous settlements on Thwaites Fell and Corney Moor. Few of the South Cumberland hut circles have been dug, and the only really important find is the urn found near the Beck, Millom, about 1872, and now at Broadgate. It is a beautiful piece of work, 10½ inches high with a diameter of 8½ inches across the top The upper half is decorated by two bands, the upper ornamented by a cord pattern made by impressing twisted thongs in the moist clay, the lower by incised lines. The diameter of the urn below this ornament is 9 inches and from this point it slopes to a base of 4½ inches.

The Bronze Age people lived on farming and hunting until they learnt the use of iron. A second wave of Keltic invaders, the iron-using Brythons arrived in Britain about B.C. 800, but did not penetrate the north-western fells, so the Romans found a Goidelic race still inhabiting these regions.

The megalithic remains of South Cumberland are known to us largely by report, for most have been removed in the course of cultivation. Only one stone remained in 1794 of the Annaside circle ; formerly there had been a circle of 12, having a diameter of 20 yards. About a quarter of a mile from Hall Foss were 8 " massive columns " forming a circle of 25 yards diameter known as Standing Stones. At Gutterby were 30 stones arranged in two concentric circles, the inner being almost complete in 1800. This was the largest of all the South Cumberland circles. The Giant's Grave at Kirksanton is mentioned in 1309 as " the two standing stones;" they are 15 feet apart, 10 and 8 feet high respectively, and on the higher are cup markings. Not far from the Giant's Grave and about 500 feet above sea level are the old housestead Lacra and the irregular heap of ruins, probably medieval, known as the Old Kirk, a rectangular platform measuring 20 yards by 50 yards once enclosed by upright shafts of stone 5 feet high. To the west is a stone and earth dyke about 4 feet broad, and not far away two circles, one of 8 and the other of 7 stones, each has a diameter of 15 yards.

To the north-east is Swinside circle, 55 stones set in close order in beds of smaller stones, there is a gateway to the south-east. On the Mount, near Ash House, there are two stones about 3 feet high, traces of others show it to be the lost circle mentioned by Hutchinson; like Swinside this circle has a diameter of 100 feet.

These circles can be divided into Large and Small stone types. The large stone type such as Swinside belongs to the Stone Age. Of their use we know nothing. They are not burial grounds, excavation at Swinside produced nothing but a century old Lancaster halfpenny, they must have been tribal meeting places. The circles of small stones are of the Bronze Age and are mostly fences of interments; some are of great area and contain several tumuli. To sum up, Neolithic man lived upon the coast strip and rarely penetrated far inland; men of the Bronze Age inhabited the upland moors and left a band of remains that stretches from Furness to Solway. It seems highly probable that the present roads from Swinside over Thwaites Fell and Corney Fell, through Barnscar and over Burnmoor into Wasdale, linking up cairns and hut circles, belong to prehistoric days.

There are but slight traces of the Roman occupation in the Millom district. Agricola passed through it on his march north in A.D. 78. The Roman road from Ambleside to Ravenglass over Wrynose practically follows the course of the modern road; it crossed the Duddon at Cockley

Beck, perhaps went to Black Hall and thence to Hardknott
with its fort following the thirteenth century Wainsgarth
whose course can still be traced.

The next invaders were the Anglians, who came by
the Wall, the Irthing Valley and Stainmoor. The early
form of some of the place names points to a settlement
in the early seventh century, perhaps under Ethelfrith, at
any rate the colonization of Furness seems later than 685,
when King Egfrith gave St. Cuthbert " the land called
Cartmel and all the Britons with it." The newcomers
settled in the lowland plains about Whicham, Millom,
Bootle and Kirksanton, but left no trace save in their place
names.

Three centuries later another wave of Teutonic migra-
tion flooded the district with Vikings, Norsemen who sailed
from the fjords of Norway down the west coast of Scotland
or crossed from Ireland, arriving in this district about 925
and gradually working their way up the valleys.

A chief would establish his " bær " or " by " in an
accessible place near the mouth of a river, as we may
suppose Ornulf did at Arnaby, then his thralls took his
sheep and cattle to summer pastures, " sætr " or " ergs,"
further up amongst the hills. Often these dairies have
Gaelic personal names from the Scotch and Irish thralls
who founded them ; naturally they tended to become in
time fixed farms. Remains of these shielings are to be
found on Thwaites Fell. Further up a valley is usually a
name beginning with grise or swin(e), showing that pigs
roamed the forest ; even in the twelfth century there are
frequent references to pannage of swine in these uplands,
and Swinside stands at the head of a valley. The Norse
found Britons still inhabiting the lower fells, as the name
Birkby, the village of the Britons, shows. The harassed
Cymric government took the Norse as their allies, the races
intermarried ; the only memorial these Kelts have left us
is a few river names, sheep scoring numerals and the many
hut-circles and cairns upon lonely moors.

The Northmen left a deep impression upon Cumberland. Most of its place names are Norse, and its dialect

is but a development of a Norse language spoken here until the thirteenth century, " so sharp, harsh, grating and formless," says a writer in 1125. The parallel development of Norse in Cumberland and Norway resulted in similar words such as *gimmer lamb, attercob* and *fremmed* being found in both languages. The Cumbrian " reckling," weakest of a litter or brood, is the Icelandic *recklingr*, " sackless," simple, corresponds to *saklauss*, and " handsel," bargain, to *handsal*.

The following are the most interesting of the local place names. O.N. and O.E. are used for Old Norse and Old English respectively.

ARNABY *(Arnolveby*, 1230), the byr or farm of Ornulfr.

BIRKBY *(Bretteby*, 1272), O.N. Brettebyr, the Britons' village.

BOOTLE *(Bodele*, 1186), O.E. buthl, buildings.

BORWICK RAILS *(Burghwick*, 1741), O.E. berewick, demesne farm.

CHAPEL SUCKEN *(Sooken*, 1725), O.N. sogn, district, cf. Norw. Sognekirk, parish.

DUDDON *(Dudenam, Duden*, 12th cent.), Old Brit. river name ident. with *Dubo, black and O.E. denu, valley.

DUNNINGWELL *(Dunningkeld*, 1210), O.E. pers. n. Dunn, O.N. kelda, spring.

GREEN, in the eighteenth century and earlier this was Rally Green.

HAVERIGG *(Haverig*, 1180), O.N. hafri-hryggr, the ridge of oats.

HESTHAM *(Hestholm*, 1279), the holm upon which horses (O.N. hestr) pasture.

HOUBERGH, 1338, Borwick Rails. O.N. the hill shieling.

KIRKSANTON *(Sancta Cherche*, D.B., *Kirchesanton*, 1170), Church of St. Sanctan, an Irish saint.

LACRA *(Lowcray*, 1404), O.N. laug and vra, hollow among the hills.

LANGTHWAITE *(Langethwait)*, cf. O. Norw. Langa-
thuit, the distant thwaite.

MILLOM *(Millum, Mullum,* 1190; *Myllum,* 1228), O.E.
mylnum, the mills, is a philologically
sound explanation. The topographers, who can find no site for mills,
propose O.N. melum, the sandhills
or meals, and explain the early forms
by supposing confusion with the
word for mills; other cases of iden-
tical confusion are known, but the
early forms of Millom show no such
confusion as do the forms quoted by
the topographers, e.g., Milburn,
Westmorland.

ULPHA *(Ulfhou,* 1337), Ulf's How or hill.

WHICHAM *(Witingham,* D.B.), the homestead of the
Hvitingas.

The next few years of Cumbrian history are highly
obscure, indeed, well-authenticated history is lacking until
the time of Henry I. Although the Vikings aided the
Cumbri, there can be little doubt that when in 966 Thored
of York harried Westmorland, and in 1000, when Ethelred
despoiled Cumberland, it was to keep down the restless,
raiding Norse.

At the time of the Conquest it is probable that there
were churches at Waberthwaite, Bootle, and Whicham,
perhaps also at Millom, indeed, there are two strong argu-
ments in favour of this view. Soon after 1086 the church
at Kirksanton is referred to as a daughter church of Millom;
in addition the income of the Norman church at Millom
was rectoral, held by the Lord of Millom, who granted it
away, Saxon fashion, not by right of his seigniory, but
rather as a lay priest. Near the church is a field, Childrum,
and this has been suggested to be a survival of the Gaelic,
Cill-dhruin, the ridge of the chapel.

Before the Conquest the Millom district was included
in the Earldom of Northumbria held by Tostig. North of

this vague line the volatile Gospatric was in possession. At the Norman Conquest Cumberland was formally removed from the lordship of Scotland to that of England, but until about 1080 it was probably almost a separate kingdom, stretching from the Clyde to the Duddon. William seems to have valued it but lightly and to have left its recovery to his followers. The Doomsday Book survey does not deal with Cumberland save for Tostig's former manors. The entry reads, " The King's Land in Euric Scire, West Reding, Agemundrenesse. M(anor) In Hougun earl Tostig had 4 carucates of land for geld, 4 carucates in Witingham, 4 carucates in Bodele, 1 carucate in Sancta Cherche, 6 in Hougenai. All these vills lie near to Hougun." It was formerly thought that Hougun was Millom, but the general opinion to-day is that High Haume, in Furness, is meant.

2.—THE LORDS OF MILLOM.

OF the first Normans in South Cumberland little is known. Roger de Poictou, to whom William gave all the land in Lancashire, looms through the mists, and is said to have invaded Cumberland; perhaps Gospatrick had attempted to extend his domain to the Duddon. Roger in his Lancashire lands adopted a firm attitude and placed his chief tenants at points which commanded fords; Millom, if he ever troubled to extend his rights, was probably no exception. The date of the acquirement of Jura Regalia by Millom is unknown; in 1292 the Lords are said to have exercised the right of gallows time out of mind. These considerations, together with the probability of a pre-Norman church, seem to support the existence of a motte near the Millom ford.

In the reign of William Rufus, Ranulf le Meschyn was placed in charge of the frontier district; when he married Lucia, daughter of Ivo Tailbois, is not known, but she received, either then or soon after, the land between Esk and Duddon. William Meschyn went on a crusade, perhaps as representative of his brother, Ranulf; with him would go his feudal dependents, among them Godard, chief tenant of Lucia for the Manor of Millom. Godard seems to have rendered some signal service, and on his return was rewarded by Ranulf with the Lordship of the four South Cumberland manors with all rights which Tostig, Roger, Ivo, and Lucia had possessed.

The Conquest thus means for Cumberland the invasion of 1092 by William II and the creation of the fort of Carlisle. The land between Duddon and Esk reverted to the Scotch crown, though inhabited by English and ruled by Normans. Under David I. of Scotland the land was owned by William Meschyn, brother of Ranulf, Lord of Carlisle, and later of Chester. William died in 1134, and

Alice de Rumelli carried the Barony of Egremont and Lordship of Skipton to her husband, William Fitz Duncan, nephew of David, king of Scotland. When Stephen usurped the English throne, David entered England in 1138 with an army, and Fitz Duncan was at the head of an expedition which ravaged his own inheritance in Cumberland and Craven. The monks were driven from Calder and the Abbey land of Furness plundered. In 1294 John Balliol, King of Scotland, stayed at Bootle on his way south to London.

The Norman development of the district included the foundation of St. Bees Priory in 1125 by William Meschyn with the help of his feudal dependents. It was given to St. Mary's, York, and although destroyed by the Scots in 1315, was, at the time of the dissolution, the third richest house in Cumberland. In 1123 Stephen, not yet King, gave land near Preston to the Norman-French Abbey of Savigny. A colony of monks was sent over, but stayed only three years, for the same donor, in 1127, gave them the whole of Furness, excluding the le Fleming lands. Here they built their Abbey and followed the Benedictine rule until 1148, when they were transferred to the Cistercian order.

In the following lists each lord is the son of the preceding lord unless otherwise stated.

A.—THE BOYVILS OF MILLOM.

1. **Godard de Boyvil** (b. c. 1075) is the first of whom we have any knowledge. In one of his charters he refers to his father as the holder of Foss, or the larger part of Whitbeck. When William Meschyn founded St. Bees Priory Godard gave to it the Churches of Whicham and Bootle with their parishes, tithes, and parsonages for the purpose of providing lights. This is interesting as an early example of fully equipped parishes. He also gave a carucate of land in Foss to Furness in 1135, probably when he was on his deathbed. His widow, Mahild, gave St Bees a farm in Annaside.

2. **Arthur de Boyvil** (d. c. 1184) was a minor at his father's death. He confirmed the gift of Robert, his cousin, of Kirksanton and Horrum to Furness. In 1182 he rendered account for enquiry into his right of one knight's fee against the Countess of Copeland.

3. **Henry de Boyvil,** who married Godith, is not remarkable for his religious benefactions. When William, son of Waldeve, married his daughter Alice, he gave him " a messuage, croft and garden formerly held by Leuenad the Fowler and 6 acres of land next to Lairpul." William and his wife and their heirs were to be free of multur and panage, but their tenants were to pay one-fifteenth for multur (miller's toll) and one-twentieth for pannage. This land is probably part of Helpa Bridge Farm. In addition, they received an acre of meadow " near the spring of Holy Trinity as the road lies towards Thwaites, namely, an acre near the marsh road." There are said to have been two Holy Wells at Millom, one near Hodbarrow, the other inside the embankment between the Gallows and Burn-field, once used as a purge. The description in the deed seems to point along the Thwaites road; if so, the Deer-leap or Pennypot Well is likely. Henry had a nephew, William, who gave land at Dunningwell to Furness, and a daughter, Gunhild, who received as marriage portion land in Leakley, now Seaton, which she gave on her husband's death to Holm Cultram Abbey.

4. **William de Boyvil** (d. c. 1227) gave to Furness the advowson of Holy Trinity, Millom, with all its chapels, also the saltworks near Lairwath that Nigel had held, together with 4 acres of arable land and all other appur-tenances in lands, fisheries, sands and mosses, together with sufficient peat rights to maintain the salt works, and common rights in all the common pasture of Millom for 8 oxen, 4 cows and 2 horses. The Kirksanton salinae appear to have been on the low ground near Helpa Bridge. Three things were necessary for saltworks : peat, fresh water, and ready access to the shore. The salt water was caught in shallow pans divided by clay walls and evap-

orated, the rough sand was then scraped up and placed in a higher tank and the process repeated. This rough mixture of sand and salt was then carted to the works by draught oxen or horses, pasture for which appears in the grants. This sludge was placed in wooden troughs with bottoms pierced by fine holes, fresh water was then poured in carrying the salt to the brine pits, where by evaporation and the constant addition of fresh brine it became highly impregnated. The final stage was in the boiling house, where after several hours' boiling, the salt began to corn ; it was then raked out and placed in creels to dry in a warm compartment through which the flues passed. The salinae probably continued, as elsewhere, into the sixteenth cen- tury when a coast trade of cod and herrings developed with Liverpool and Chester, and the boats returned with salt.

5. **Adam de Boyvil** was the brother of William. In 1230 he released all rights in the advowson of Millom to Furness, and about the same time granted to St. Bees a salinae in Millom and a hearth for it near Slepul, or as it is now known, High Shaw Pool ; the boundaries extended towards Roanlands. Peat and pasture rights were also granted and leave to build saltworks and houses from the donor's woods.

6. **Joan de Boyvil,** Adam's heir, married John de Hudleston, and thus the Boyvil period ended.

B.—THE LORDS OF KIRKSANTON.

The Kirksanton Manor House is traditionally supposed to have been Garthlands, but certain charters make it probable that it was upon the Green where, it is stated, the Church once stood.

1. **Robert de Boyvil** (d. c. 1158) went on a pilgrim- age, probably the Crusade of 1146, and left all his land of Kirksanton and Horrum to the monks of Furness in such a way that he should on his return be again a free tenant.

This gift was subsequently confirmed by his cousin, Arthur,
Lord of Millom.   Horrum is a little way below Wains-
gate Bridge at a point where by two angles the stream
partly encloses a group of 12 fields, now called Huron or
Youren.

2.   **William de Boyvil** (d. c. 1170) granted to Furness
the Meles of Kirksanton, about 25 acres lying close to the
parish boundary between Layriggs and Southfield, also to
the monks dwelling within the bounds as much wood as
they required from his wood, together with a moiety of
the fishing in Helupul (Whicham Beck), free grinding of
their corn at his mill and the rights of sea-wreckage along
the shore within certain bounds.   He later added the
Holm (Monksholm to-day) and 10 acres near the Millom
Boundary " for the soul of my son Radulf " and for the
support of the Secular Infirmary of Furness.

3.   **Robert de Boyvil** (d. c. 1183) married Margaret,
daughter of Waldeve ; one of their sons, Richard, held a
moiety of the Rectory of Whicham, and about 1186 gave
10 acres of land in Caldreton to Calder Abbey.   Gilbert,
another son, gave to Cockersand Abbey 3 acres of land
in Haverigg and two in Wrang or Wringes, which appears
in the Parish Register 1604-72 as Ringes belonging to a
family called Myre.   A cottager attached to the farm died
at the age of 111 in 1633.   Wringes was part of Huron.

4.   **William de Boyvil** (d. c. 1210).   Late in the
twelfth century Cecily, Countess of Albemarle, gave 4
carucates in Kirksanton with the services of William de
Boyvil to St. Mary's, York.   Clement, Abbot of York,
released Kirksanton to William, who pledged himself to
pay half-a-mark yearly, and named his brothers Gilbert
and Robert and his nephew Henry as guarantees.   Though
there is no direct evidence to prove the de Boyvils and
the de Levingtons were connected, it appears probable
that this was so.   The following three lords of Kirksanton,
Sir Guy, Sir William, and John are contemporary with Sir
Guy, Sir William and John de Levington.   Ranulph

Meschyn had given the barony of Levington to Richard
de Boyvil before Godard received the Honour of Millom.

5. **Sir Guy de Boyvil** (d.c. 1256) seems to have been
much absent from Kirksanton, his place being taken by
his brother, John de Boyvil, who had married his cousin
Ellen of Langthwaite, and possessed in his own right a
great deal of land in the district.   The Manor of Kirksanton consisted then of the township of Chapel Sucken
with the exception of Hestholm.   The estate had been
diminished by gifts made from time to time and by an
annuity to St. Bees secured by lease and release.

6. **Sir William de Boyvil** (d. 1305) in 1288 released
the whole Manor to St. Bees Priory, mills, lands and all
liberties, and seems to have left the district.   He was sued
for service due by Sir Hudleston in 1276.

7. **John de Boyvil** (d. 1319).   At his death it was
reputed that he held the Manor from the Abbot of St.
Mary's, and that there was no capital messuage in the
Manor because it had been burnt by the Scots, perhaps
during their raid in 1316.

8. **Edmund de Boyvil,** brother of John, succeeded at
the age of 30, and sold all the lands to Andrew Harcla.

C.—THE HUDLESTONS.

The Hudlestons derive their name from a village in
Yorkshire, the original family of Sherburn in Elmet runs :
I. NIGEL (1112-15), Praepositor to the Archbishop of
York ; II., GILBERT ; III., RICHARD (1160-90) ; IV., RICHARD
(1198-1250) ; V., RICHARD ; VI., RICHARD.

1. **John de Hudleston** (d. 1252) who married Joan
de Boyvil, was the son of Richard (IV) above. He secured
for Millom the grant of a three days annual fair at Trinity
time.   A fair was the most important franchise that could

be annexed to a manor, for there the tenants could sell their goods and buy wares they could not produce themselves. The right of holding such a fair was granted only by the king; the Lord of Millom died before paying for his privilege and his successor was sued for the money.

2. **Sir John Hudleston** (1242-1306) was a minor at his father's death and is frequently referred to as the Lord of Anneys, perhaps an estate his mother conferred upon him to give him standing. The affairs of the manor were administered by his mother and her second husband, Robert de Lathum. Sir John confirmed the gift of the Kirksanton saltworks and granted an extra pan and more peats, also, for additional brine, two acres of sands with leave to take the sand for the improvement of their own grounds. To Calder Abbey he gave rights of pasture in the common lands of Millom and two acres of land, called Sandflos, now a part of the brick and tile works field. " Furthermore they may divert the Rutandpul from the aforesaid lands free of charge." Rutandpul was the shore estuary of the Wyre, which rose near Moor Farm, once Wirehead, but whose course is now lost among the railway sidings; this is the earliest reference to the Millom saltworks, which have left their name in Salt House Farm. In 1292 he was summoned to prove his claim to such rights as were usually held by the Crown, such as free chase and gallows; this he did successfully, and the same year granted to Furness free passage by accustomed roads through all his lands save Anneys.

Sir John's life was an active one; in 1276-92 he fought in Wales, and in 1296-8 and in 1300 in Scotland, being summoned as a Baron of the Realm. Either on the way to or when returning from the Welsh War the party stayed at Furness, here his confirmation of the Kirksanton deeds and grant of common lands led to a dispute and the challenge to trial by combat of Roger of Hestholm in controvery with Furness; the contest should have taken place at Appleby but Roger withdrew. In 1302 Sir John was one of the signatories to the Barons' letter to the Pope.

Richard VI of Sherburn sold the manor of Hudleston at Sherburn to John de Melsa; in 1288 and 1290 the Millom lord had a suit with him to recover it but as the manor was handed on to Geoffrey de Melsa the suit appears to have been unsuccessful. Sir John married Sybil, probably daughter of Lawrence Cornubia, and with his wife gave lands at Richmond to his younger brother, Richard, of which lands they had been enfeoffed by Lawrence, whose grandson gave the manor of Ulverston to Sybil's son, Sir Richard. Sir John also obtained lands at Whittington, Lancs., from Alan de Coupland.

3. **Sir Richard Hudleston** (1282-1335) married Alice, supposed to be daughter of Gilbert de Colevil de Aspali, Suffolk. He was at Bannockburn, in the train of Robert de Clifford, also with Adam de Harcla at Carlisle and Boroughbridge; at the latter place he probably fought against his brother Adam. In 1323 Adam gave all his lands at Whittington and elsewhere to his brother Richard.

4. **Sir John Hudleston** (b. 1306). In 1317 his father granted Sir William Pennington " the marriage of John, his eldest son, to Maud, daughter of the said Sir William, for 250 marks and the said Sir Richard hath enfeoffed the said John and Maud in 20 marks' worth of land in the town of Bretby, Seton, Botill and Millom." It was the fourth lord who obtained the license to crenellate his house in 1335.

5. **Sir John de Hudleston,** of age 1351, is said to have married Anne Fenwick, who belonged to a powerful Northumberland family.

6. **Sir John de Hudleston** succeeded in 1377 and married Katharine (?) and died about 1397.

7. **Sir Richard de Hudleston** whilst still a minor in 1398, with others, including Richard Hudleston, of Hyton, raided Millom and expelled the servants of Robert de Harrington, knt., who " was in peaceful possession upon the death of John de Hudleston, knt." Sir Richard

married Katharine Harrington, sister of Sir William Harrington, K.G., and was present at Agincourt in 1415.

8. **Sir John Hudleston** was the grandson of Sir Richard, his father being Richard, who married Joan. In 1459 he was present at Bloreheath, but was pardoned the same year by the Coventry Parliament. In 1461 he was knighted and was Constable of Cockermouth (1460-72) It appears that in 1460 Millom Castle was badly damaged by the Lancastrians. Sir John was present at Bosworth in 1485 on the side of Richard III, and after the battle he and his son Henry seem to have been in hiding, for they were summoned to come in; they did so and were pardoned. He held many important offices and was deputy Warden of the Western Marches for Richard III. After 1472 he seems to have gone to Cambridgeshire and to have lived pretty continuously at court. He was very successful in obtaining heiresses for his sons; Richard married a natural daughter of Warwick the Kingmaker, Margaret Nevill; William married Isabel Nevil, daughter of Mantague; and John, Joan Stapleton, daughter and co-heiress of Sir Miles Stapleton and widow of Christopher Harcourt. He died in 1494 and his sandstone altar tomb remains in Millom Castle with the Hudleston arms and those of his wife, Mary Fenwick, at the head, and those of his sons and daughters on each side.

9. **Richard Hudleston,** grandson of the Yorkist and son of Sir Richard (d. 1484) and Margaret Nevill, was seized at Whittington by Lady Mabel Dacre and married to her daughter, Elizabeth. For this forcible marriage of a king's ward Lady Mabel was imprisoned in Harbottle Castle, and her daughter, for whose sake she was incarcerated, died in the Castle whilst attending her mother. Richard himself died before 1509. He is commemorated by the alabaster altar tomb in Millom Church.

10. **Sir John Hudleston** (d. 1512), son of the Yorkist, married Joan Stapleton and spent his life in Gloucestershire as Constable of Sudeley Castle and Sheriff of Glou-

THE HUDLESTON ALABASTER TOMB

cester. In his will he regrets inducing his wife, contrary
to the " olde intailes," to leave her estate to their son,
and directs that she leave it to the issue of her first marriage ; her son, John, however, did succeed to the Yorkshire estate. He also orders that " there be leyde upon
me a stone of marble with a picture of myself sett therein
and writing thereuppon to make mencion of me and of my
departinge," and desires to be buried at Hayles Abbey,
should he die near it ; his wish appears to have been
fulfilled.

11. **Sir John Hudleston** (1488-1547) built Southam
Hall in Gloucestershire and appears to have left Millom to
the care of his Steward, William Latus, who succeeded in
marrying his son, Ralph, to Sir John's daughter, Anne.
Sir John gave his support to the Reformed Religion, and
was present at the marriage of Anne Boleyn. He himself
married three times : his first wife, Jane Clifford, died child-
less ; his second, Joan Seymour, had a son, Anthony, who
carried on the Millom line ; and his third, Joyce Prickley,
another, Andrew, who founded the Hutton John family.

12. **Anthony Hudleston** (1519-1598) married Mary
Barrentine, afterwards quarrelling with her and her brothers. Before his death he attempted to disinherit his son
William, who, however, succeeded in securing the Millom
title deeds and thus successfully proved his claim to
succeed.

13. **William Hudleston** (d. 1628) was brought up at
his mother's place, Great Haseley, Oxfordshire, to which,
as well as Millom and Cothurston, he succeeded. He married Mary Bridges, of Gloucestershire, and had fifteen
children. His three grandsons, by Anthony, all met
violent deaths : one at Marston Moor, another at Bowden
Moor, and the third in Scotland. He was known as a great
swashbuckler and gamester and saddled the estate with
heavy debts, increased by his son and heir.

The following is an extract from William's will :

" I give to my eldest sonne ffardinando my whyte
stoud horse. Item to my daughter in lawe his wife
fortie shillings to make her a Ringe. Item I give unto
my sonne Anthonie tenne sheape and to his wife tenne
sheape. Item I give unto my sonne Barantino the
elder one horse. Item to my sonne Lamploughe my
Armenige sword. Item to my daughter Elizabeth my
velvet gowne. Item I give unto my eldest daughter
my arrearages due unto me by Anthonie Dale according to my letter to her under my hand. Item I give unto
her more one Cowe. Item I give to my daughter Latus
fortie shillinges to make her a Ringe. . . Item I give
to my Sonne Thomas Hudleston and my three daughters ffrances Albina and Jane all my rents and arrearages of Rents due unto me by ffardinando my eldest
sonne for my forge in Vlfay for and during all the
time since he first entered into the same being three
hundred pounds by yeare. . . .

Given under my hand this Tenthe daie of June
anno Dmi 1625. William Hudleston. Item I give
unto my eldest daughter Mary more one hundrethe
pownds to be paid her by my eldest sonne out of the
arrearages which are due to me for the upper forge."

14. **Ferdinand Hudleston** (d. c. 1645) married a
daughter of Sir Ralph Grey, of Chillingham, and also had
fifteen children, including ten sons ; one died aged 10
months, the other nine served in the Royalist army.
Richard, a Lt.-Col of Foot, was killed in the Minster Yard
at York. In 1622, before his father's death, Ferdinand
was granted a license to crenellate, this probably means
that after a period of absenteeism the Castle required over-
hauling, though it has been suggested that the Tower may
be a freak building of this date. In 1625 the whole of the
Millom estates were re-settled on the sons, Cothurston
and Romaldkirk being used to provide dowers for the
wives, Jane and Bridget. Ferdinand was practically a
pensioner on his wife and son.

15. **Col. Sir William Hudleston** (1603-68) was the well-known Cavalier. He married Bridget Pennington, of Muncaster. He raised, paid and clothed a Royalist regiment. In June, 1643, the Parliamentarians, under Col. Rigby, arrived in Lancashire to raise forces in Leyland and Amounderness Hundreds to reduce Thurland Castle ; in August they marched against it and a seven weeks' siege resulted. During this period they were harried by Cumberland and Westmorland Royalists under Col. Hudleston, Roger Kirkby, and Alexander Rigby of Burgh, so that when Rigby heard that Hudleston had gathered a force of 1,600 men in Furness, things grew serious, and leaving just sufficient men to blockade Thurland he marched thirty miles in a day and reached Ulverston at night. The next morning after prayers at Swarthmoor, he met the Royalists at Lindale-in-Furness. Rigby had a superior force, including 500 foot, three troops of horse and two guns, and at his first charge the Royalists began to retreat, a quarter of an hour later they were in full flight. Cavalry in pursuit captured Col. Hudleston, Mr. Stanley, and Mr. Latus, of Beck, together with between 300 and 400 men, Mr. Lewthwaite, of Millom, being killed. Rigby's despatch concludes : " because Colonel Hudleston (who yet hath a regiment in Yorkshire, in or near Halifax) is as I heare Serjeant Major Generall of Cumberland ; and the most considerable man in Cumberland. . . . and one whom without further danger to the peace of our countie, I cannot conceive can be kept prisoner here. I have there-presumed to send him to you." On hearing of this disaster Thurland surrendered.

After Marston Moor Prince Rupert went by the Yorkshire Dales into Lancashire. Sir John Meldrum was therefore sent from York with 1,000 men to clear the county ; on hearing of his approach the Royalists retreated into Fylde, but some under Col. Hudleston, brother of Sir William, and Lord Ogleby, attempted to reach the shelter of Lathom House, which had been turned over to Rupert after the first siege, but were met by Col. Dodding near Walton. The Royalists had 400 horse and outnumbered Dodding, but word was sent to Col. Shuttleworth near Blackburn, he hastened to the scene and the Royalists were routed, among the 50 prisoners being both Col. Hudleston and Lord Ogleby. It is interesting to note that our main authority for the siege of Lathom is the Journal of the chaplain, Rutter, who assisted the Countess de Trémouille. Rutter had, in 1630, been presented to the living of Waberthwaite by Joseph Pennington, and was again presented in 1641 by William Pennington. He was a confidential friend of the seventh Earl of Derby and became a Canon of Lichfield, and finally, in 1661, Bishop of Sodor and Man.

Millom Castle was besieged and held out obstinately in 1644; nothing is known of the siege, but tradition has it that the Parliamentarian cannon were placed on the Knott, above Low House, also at Warr Knotts, a mile due north. The Vicarage, which stood near the Castle, is said to have been pulled down so that it should not harbour rebels.

Sir William's imprisonment apparently did not last long, for in 1648 he was at Cockermouth with his son Ferdinand, as the following letter shows:

" Petition of Richard Uriell and Thomas Crosthwaite late merchants of Cockermouth to the Protector. In 1648 by order of Maj. Gen. Lambert we assisted the late Major William Bird to defend Cockermouth Castle on a three months' siege by Sir Wm. Hudleston who totally plundered our estate value £1965 by which we have been disabled to maintain ourselves."

Then followed the sequestration of the Millom estate. Hudleston's fine was set at a moiety of £2,212 in May, 1647. Three years later he begs to compound for delinquency in arms in both wars, and in November the fine was advanced to £2,242 10s. In 1654 he petitioned Cromwell for a remission of the remainder of his fine, which for both wars, he says, ought to have been only £1,492. Later in the year the committee considered the fines due out of the estate pardoned. In 1655 special taxes were laid upon delinquents to raise money for the Militia Troop. Hudleston's £55 is the highest assessment in Cumberland.

In 1666, after his marriage, Ferdinand, Sir William's heir, solicited Daniel Fleming for help against his father, who, he says, "came with a companie of rude and manie of them Outlawed persons with guns and swordes and other weapons and threatened to turn me out and hath wounded some of my men . . . and he hath got into an outhouse close by me and saies he will starve me out being more in number than I am and will not suffer anye to come at me, and I can not subsist till to-morrow at night for want of vittayles." Accordingly, Sir Daniel wrote to the constables of Millom commanding them to aid him " untill he shall bee thence ejected by due course of Law. And hereof fail not at your perill."

Sir Daniel Fleming also records the appearance in 1665 off Millom of some Dutch privateers, which caused alarm in the district. " Young Joseph Hudleston a trained band Captain under Sir George Fletcher," raised the countryside ; this was the second of Sir William's sons.

In addition to the fines and charges imposed by the Commonwealth there was a charge of £2,000 to provide marriage portions for his daughters to come out of the Millom estates ; all the daughters died except one, Joyce, who claimed the whole sum, the result was numerous Chancery suits. A year before his father's death there is a letter from Ferdinand to Williamson in which he desires to become king's servant to preserve his person for a hearing of his cause before the Lord Chamberlain with reference to a debt for which he is bound with his father, £1,000 has been paid, but the claimant still demands the original sum. Sir William Hudleston died in a debtors' prison at Carlisle in 1668 and was buried at Millom.

The Hospital at Whitbeck was built by the parishioners themselves at Moor Green and was endowed, about 1630, with £400 by Henry Parke, a mercer of Kendal, who was born at Whitbeck. In 1639 the trustees invested this money in an annual rent charge of £24 from William and Bridget Hudleston, to be paid out of the Scoggarbar estate and out of a messuage and tenement, Crosbythwaite, in Ulpha.   The Ulpha lands were discharged from payment in 1744 and by indenture of the same date, Edward Gibson, one of the trustees, purchased Scoggarbar from William Hudleston and the payment fell upon his estate at Middlefoss.

16. **Ferdinand Hudleston** (1607-86) married a London heiress, Dorothy Hewkley, and appears to have paid the fines and occupied the Castle, doing some slight restoration ; he may have built the entrance steps, repaired the Pele and inserted the main oak staircase.   He contemplated entering Parliament, for there is a letter from his wife to Sir Daniel Fleming, soliciting his aid.   Ferdinand's Royalist election address was issued as a broadside : " The Speech of Ferdinando Huddleston, Esq., in the face of the County.   At the Election at Baggry, in the County of Cumberland, the 27 day of August, 1679 . . . I here declare in the face of the County I come here to the assistance of our King and Country and to uphold the most glorious Church in the world, setled in this Isle."   He failed, and petitioned against the return, but did not prosecute his petition.   But Ferdinand, like his father, died in prison, the King's Bench Prison, Southwark.   He had endeavoured to repay his debts by mortgages, entailed property, and by trying to develop the iron industry in the district. His unfortunate wife became a lunatic.

17. **Joseph Hudleston** (d. 1700) was the brother of Ferdinand, who had left only a daughter, who married the Earl Delawar.   He married Bridget Hudleston, of Hutton John, and she seems to have brought some relief for a time from the pressing financial burden.   Joseph left £100 to found a school at Millom.

18. **Richard Hudleston** (d. 1718) was the next heir, as Joseph died without issue.   He was the son of Col. John Hudleston, of Longarth, Ulpha, the brother of Col. Sir

William, the fifteenth lord. When Richard came into
possession Bridget had to sue for her dower, and eventually parted, leaving all she could to her sister Mary, wife
of John Senhouse, of Netherhall, whose son, Humphrey,
had been brought up at the Castle. Richard was twice
married, first to Isobel Hudleston, of Bainton, and after
her death to Bridget, widow of William Kirkby, and
daughter of John Latus, of Beck.

19. **Ferdinand Hudleston** (1673-1730) married Elizabeth Faulkner, of Guppington, Rutland, and left a debt
of £9,000 upon the estate.

20. **William Hudleston** (1698-1745) married Gertrude
Meredith, daughter of Sir William Meredith, Cheshire. He
appears from his will to have quarrelled violently with his
wife and her relations, since he forbids either of his
daughters in his will to live with their mother. He left the
same debt upon the estate.

21. **Elizabeth Hudleston** married Sir Hedworth
Williamson, who sold the Millom estate to Sir James
Lowther, of Whitehaven, for £20,000. A private Act of
Parliament had to be obtained to free the entail and allow
the proceeds to be used to pay the debts of the last two
lords.

The following is from an inventory, dated 2/10/1574,
of the goods of Bernard Hudleston, of the Whicham and
Kirksanton branch of the family :—

Impms.	VI oxen Vº Kyne Vº younge beastes	XVI		
Itm.	XXXIII Shepe oulde and younge	III	X	
	VI Swyne		X	
	XVIIII gese oulde and younge		VI	VIII
	XI Stacke of wheate		XLVII	VIII
	IX busshelles of Rye		XXXVI	
	in otes	IX	III	IIII
	One marser¹ and a horne		XXVI	VIII
	IIIº payre of shetes		VII	IIII

IIIᵒ coverlette and IIIᵒ happinge[2]	XIIII		IIII
One candlestycke and schomer[3]			
one Chafyndishe[4]	III		
IIIᵒ brass pottes	XVI		
in pannes	XI		
one Cowdren[5]	VI		
One greate brasse potte	XII		
one gyrdle branderethe[6] and Chyrset	II	IIII	
IIᵒ spetes and one tryppet[7]	II	VIII	
in woddne wessell	VI	VIII	
VI teannes IIᵒ hatchytte one gavelock[8]	XII		
in spades and II . . . se teames	IIII	VIII	
in wolle and yearne	V	IIII	
hempe and Lyne			XVI
in Chistes and Arkes	XXII		
VI Hennes			XVI
IIᵒ bordes and formes	III	VI	
IIᵒ Drinkpottes			VIII
VIII yockes IIᵒ harrowes and one payre of qweles[9]	IIII		
in saddles	IIII		
IIᵒ plowes and a Care	III		
one wayne and one Carte	V		

Somme totalis	XLVI	XV	VI

1. A bason or large bowl.
2. Cover or quilt.
3. Skimmer.
4. A vessel containing charcoal for keeping cooked dishes warm.
5. Cauldron.
6. Iron frame to hold baking plate.
7. Turnspit and dish.
8. Crowbar.
9. Wheels.

III.—CHURCHES AND CHAPELS.

THE Parish Church of Holy Trinity dates back to the Norman period ; if there was an earlier church upon the present site nothing remains of it to-day. It has been assumed that the present chancel formed the original chapel because of its great length, the nave being added later and a chancel arch built between the two, but this is an unwarrantable assumption, for there are many Norman churches in which the proportion of chancel length to nave length is greater than at Millom. We may safely assume that the present chancel and nave are of the same date. The church has been repaired, improved and restored so much that it is difficult to reconstruct the original building, but to the earliest period must be assigned the beautifully splayed window in the north wall of the chancel, three similar window heads are built into the different walls of the church. There are in the south wall of the chancel a very rough aumbry niche and a piscina, unornamented save for a slight chamfer around the arched stone covering it : these may be from some earlier church. The chancel arch and the north doorway are Norman.

During the recent restoration fragments of a cross shaft and head were found in the north wall of the chancel, their workmanship suggests a late eleventh century date. On one edge of the shaft there is a cable moulding, whilst one face is decorated with a motive of Stafford knots in double row, the central lines passing through a rhomboid buckle. The head was apparently of the wheel head type, the armless centre has a central boss surrounded by criss-cross line forming no pattern but giving the effect of plait work. A freestone slab was also brought to light from the same wall, on one of its longer edges is inscribed ANTEF ; Mr. R. G. Collingwood suggests that it is Roman and suggests a reading CUR[ANTE F]LAVIO, or some such

name, the person in charge of a piece of construction being
often mentioned in late inscriptions. Considering that all
the freestone for the church was brought into the district,
we cannot be sure that the cross originally belonged to
Millom, but in 1917 a cross socket was found in the church
yard. At each corner is a roughly carved figure, the most
distinct is that of a man with folded hands, another is
bearded but part of the beard and hands has gone, but
there is a suggestion of shoulders.

Owing to the ravages of the Scots there was a drop
of three-quarters in the church revenue in 1336 as com-
pared with 1291. After this period, under the influence of
the Hudlestons, Millom began to grow in size and importance and changes naturally took place in the church.
About 1340 the old south wall of the nave was removed
and the arcade of three pointed arches was inserted and
the Hudleston Chapel built ; a piscina remains to-day near
the altar. In making the arcade part of the chancel wall
was removed and the chancel arch readjusted to spring
from the new pier, and thus ceased to be central to the
nave and chancel. In the east wall of the chapel they
built the window which seems so disproportionate to the
size of the wall and is perhaps later in date than the three
windows in the south wall. High in the west wall of the
Hudleston Chapel is the Vesica Window, known better
as the Fish or Fluke Window ; there are examples of these
windows in other churches, but that at Millom is remarkable for its size, 10ft. 4ins. by 7ft. The window was filled
with stained glass by the Rev. J. M. Lowther, Vicar of
Whicham (1862-74), but the beauty of the window lies
in its tracery rather than in its glass.

Just before the outbreak of the Civil War the Church
had been flagged by " Anthony Myre and his fellows ;"
during the siege of the Castle in 1644 the Hudleston Chapel
seems to have been almost wrecked, the east window
much broken, the side windows and the Fluke Window
smashed and their tracery broken, and the niche above
the north door robbed of its image. After this a period
of depression set in and the Church was left more and

more to the care of the parishioners. The side windows were blocked up, one being used as a doorway and another as a convenient place for the erection of a monument to the memory of Joseph and Bridgett Hudleston. There was at one time a Rood Loft, a beam across the chancel arch on which was a figure of Christ on the cross attended by the Virgin and St. John, which was mended in 1633 and again in 1701.

The Church has been whitewashed and plastered in places, a gallery was erected for the choir and the barrel organ, beneath it sat the inmates of the Hall Bank Workhouse. Later the gallery was removed to make more room. During the 1858 restoration the small square window which lighted the gallery was walled up, the oak seats taken out and the present deal pews substituted; part of the roof had been ceiled to prevent draughts, but this was removed in 1856. The floor was also raised to the height of the first chancel step on account of the damp. In 1899 the two bells were re-cast into one and the new bell turret built.

The arch in the west wall of the nave still remains a mystery; it has been suggested that it formed the entrance to a leper chapel or to a tower, also that it was built to relieve the strain upon the wall when a bell cote was built. The porch over the north door was built as a memorial to Canon Irving in 1910.

The 1930 restoration was guided by a desire to work out as far as possible the design of the fourteenth century church, which, it seems, had not been completed. The Chancel was widened and the arch recentred, the altar moved forward and the communion rails advanced and two new windows inserted in the chancel wall. The Hudleston Chapel was furnished with an altar and the western window opened and filled with clear glass. A new organ and minstrels' gallery have been placed at the west end of the nave. The original floor level has been restored, thus increasing the apparent height of the pillars and revealing the fact that the end piers of the arcade were made for a higher floor level than the three columns.

The medieval octagonal font has shields on seven sides, on the other is a large shield, partly destroyed, bearing the arms of Furness Abbey, on the left of this are Hudleston arms and on the right a shield from which the arms seem to have been effaced.

The beautifully carved alabaster altar tomb in the Hudleston Chapel commemorates the ninth lord, Richard (d. 1509) and his wife, Elizabeth Dacre. The head of the man with its long, flowing hair, rests upon a tilting helmet. He is clad in chain mail and around his neck is a collar of suns and roses, indicating his adherence to the house of York. The woman's head dress is apparently knitted, she wears a sideless côte-hardi with a long mantle. Around the tomb are niches containing figures of angels bearing plain shields and attended by small female figures kneeling and wearing the butterfly head-dress in fashion about 1460-85.

The red sandstone altar tomb is that of Sir John Hudleston and his wife, Mary Fenwick. It bears the arms of Fenwick and Hudleston at the head, around the sides those of families, including Pennington, Curwen, Nevill, and Leigh, into which members of the Hudleston family had married. On this tomb is a board for " fox and geese," cut by some impious choir boy. Before the last restoration there lay upon it a fragment of a wooden effigy, said by tradition to be " Terrible Dick ;" traces of plate armour could be seen at the knees and the feet rested upon a lion. With the shields upon the sandstone altar tomb must be taken the four on the sundial head in the church yard, two bear Hudleston arms, the others those of Chaucer and Broughton of Broughton, as the latter family became extinct in 1495 the dial cannot be much later. A sundial was once fixed upon the east buttress of the south wall, it was repaired in 1840 at a cost of 5/- and 8d. for cramps.

Two wooden pitch pipes are preserved inside the Church. In 1609 there is a registry entry, " John Greene, son of Robt. Pyper, baptised." Robert was evidently the leader of the singing and used a pipe to give the note. One is a square oak pipe bound with brass and having a mahogany air chamber and ivory mouthpiece, a brass slip at the side giving tones and semitones. The other is round and of applewood, with the notes marked by notches, evidently bought in 1826, for the Churchwardens' Accounts record, "Wm. Bleasdale and Pych pipe £1. 12. 6." These pipes fell into disuse with the introduction of the barrel organ. In 1834, 1/- was paid to someone who made a journey to enquire for a person to repair this organ, and in 1838 the organist's salary was £1 6s.

The Churchwardens' Accounts often throw light upon the life of the time. Until 1866 collections were rare at Holy Trinity and seem always to have been devoted to objects outside the parish.

1658. April 4.   ffor William Brocklebank who had lost his Killne by ffire. XVIIs.

May 2.   towards relief of the distressed church in Polande and 20 families in Bohemia. VIIIs. IVd.

1688. ffor rebuilding of ye Cathedrall Churche of St. Paules London. 00. 08. 03.

ffor ye slaves at Algeare in Turkey. 01. 02. 04.

Other entries read,

1631. Item a pelle and a seefe   04.

1694. Mowing ye weedes out of Church yard and dressing it   00. 06.

Leading 8 busshells of sand and redleing it   01. 08.

Jurny to Dalton 6d. a bell for ye sexton   01. 07.

1764. for washing church linen (for a year)   10.

It was part of the duty of the church to keep down

vermin, and payments for the heads of foxes and ravens
are a frequent item :

12 Ravens heads (Ulpha)	04.	00.
9 Fox heads	09.	00.
1656. For Killinge a Badger	03.	00.

In 1605 two sidesmen were appointed to keep dogs out
of the church " according to the canons laitly sett downe."
This was a necessary precaution when they followed their
masters, who often rode on horseback, leaving their horses
and dogs in the wooden sheds which were so frequent a
feature of church yards, including Millom.

A human note is given by the Clerk to many entries
in the registers, as when he added to the entry made in
1633 of the burial of John Murthat, of Wringes, " I hard
him say yt he was 5 score and 11 years of age," or added
to the bare fact of the burial of Henry Brocklebank in
1711 that he was " the Left Handed ffidler." In 1636 is a
rather mysterious entry, " Myles Drinkall (elder) de Way-
side, buried in a bread kind for a ten weekes." Accidents
crossing the sands were frequent. In 1792 Mary Askew,
midwife, of Moore, and in 1727 Francis Roudey, a tide-
waker at Duddon (that is a person who " brogged " the
sands with branches) were drowned, whilst in 1698 James
Danson, of Little Langthwaite, and the Vicar, the Rev.
William Wells, perished together.

In 1678 an Act was passed that every shroud must be
made of wool. The wool market was flooded, for it was
forbidden to export it, and until 1690 all burial entries
record " buried in woolen." The best local example of
a certificate is from Waberthwaite :

 " These are to certifie yt Wm Caddy of Ravenglass and ffardinando Laurence of ye same both in ye
pish of Muncaster did severally make oath before me
Sr. Wm. Pennington Barronett . . . . yt ye corps of
Edward Tubman . . . was buried . . . and was not
put in wrapt in or wound up in or buried in any shirt,

sheet or shroud made or mingled with flax hemp silk hair gold or silver or other than what was made of sheeps wool onely, or in any coffin lined or faced with any cloath, stuff or any things whatsoever than what was made of sheeps wool onely . . ''

Among the records will be found the following entries :

1605. Penance done by Janett Benson who hath had a child Jeffray Benson as was sett down by Mr. Coniston att botle the XXIII day of March Anno Dm 1595 videlicit that she should come into the Churche of Millom before morning prayer upon the Sunday next following and there confess her falt and be sorrye for her sinnes in the p'sens of sundrye psons which was done the Sunday being the XXVII day of March aforesaid in the p'sense of Christopher Askew Clerk.

1608. That Barnard Benson hathe done penance in the piche churche of Millom the XIX day of March 1608 in the presence of Christopher Askewe, Vicar of Millom and hath payed the piche church to the poor of the piche Xs which was openly delivered in the pulpit videlicit VIs VIIId. at Millum and IIIs. IIIId. at Ulfall.

1623. XIId. given to the poor of the piche by Myles Benson for sleepinge and not coming orderly to the Churche.

There was probably a church at WHICHAM as early as that at Millom. The oldest part of the present church is the unornamented twelfth century door in the south wall, around it are grooves made by the sharpening of arrows in days gone by. When the church was ceiled two feet of the east window had to be blocked up, this was done by shortening the mullions. In 1858 a transept was added. Whicham rectory was burned down by the Scots at the same time as the Battle of Scots Croft, 1322. After the dissolution of the monasteries the patronage passed into the hands of Sir Hugh Askew, of Lacra ; his widow married a Pennington.

ULPHA OLD HALL.

View and diagram of interior.

Bason Bank Farm is half in Whicham and half in Thwaites. The earliest known owners were Hodgshons (1692), one of whom married Thomas Mirfield Law, of Hestholm and Kirby Kendal, a member of the family of Law, which produced Lord Ellenborough, Lord Chief Justice in the reign of George III, a daughter, Jane, of this marriage married the Rev. Jeremiah Gilpin (1751-93) a descendant of the Apostle of the North; their daughter married George Cooper, a great-grandson of Leonard Cooper, Churchwarden of Ulpha (1718), whose name is on the bell. Later Bernard Gilpin, of Ulverston, a friend of Col. Braddyll bought many things when the latter left Conishead Priory, these included the limestone gate posts —the Gilpin Gate and the Braddyll Badger, now built in the west wall of Bason Bank.

The original parish of Millom was 35,000 acres in extent and included Kirksanton, Birker and Austhwaite. and Ulpha.

The Church of ULPHA is almost as old as that of Millom. The original church is said to have stood near the Old Hall, though it is not known when the present church was built. The old church is mentioned during the reign of Henry VIII as of the value of £5. Under the Elizabethan Poor Law Ulpha joined with Birker for the maintenance of their poor. Until 1656 the inhabitants of Birker attended Ulpha Church for sacrament and provided and paid for half the wine. The present building was formerly a mouldy, squalid, earthy-smelling place of worship, but in the last century was emptied of its ungraceful contents and refurnished in simple style. The exterior, with the exception of the porch, lych gate and belfry, remains as Wordsworth knew it, though when he visited the dale and stayed at the Kirkhouse Inn it was whitewashed both inside and out.

The Old Hall, half a mile up Holehouse Gill, is a ruined sixteenth century pele built at the very end of that tower-building period. The east wall is 6 feet thick, the lower rooms were 10 feet high, in the upper story are two fireplaces ; there are the remains of a corbel for a staircase, the ruin stands about 20 feet high. Legend says the Lady of the Hall was drowned while fleeing from a wolf in the Lady's Dub, which is near.

Frith Hall, which stands upon the hill overlooking the valley, was an ancient pack horse station, and it appears that it is the most modern representation of the manorial residence, to which Old Hall and Hall End were subsidiary. It was afterwards enlarged and used as an inn, runaway marriages were solemnised within its walls, 17 taking place in 1730.

An attempt was made at one time by Dr. Joshua King, President of Queen's College, Cambridge, to mine copper in Ulpha, but proved unsuccessful. The Millom " Gallows Stone " was erected by Dr. King.

THWAITES was a " chapel of ease " for Millom, and for a very long time had its own minister. The living was reported to Queen Anne's Bounty in 1715 as being without endowment, and five years later a grant of £200 was made to meet a similar sum raised in the parish Some authorities say the Chapel was rebuilt in 1721 and was consecrated in 1725. This chapel seated 252 persons. In 1805 a larger building was required and the old building was replaced by one more pretentious, with a steeple containing two bells, one from the old chapel with the inscription " Dixon Founder 1717," the other the gift of the Rev. John Myers, of Dunningwell. This chapel seated 350 and had a small gallery for five persons.

In 1814 the church yard was enlarged by taking in part of the school field. The few who remember this old chapel regret its removal and speak of its comfort, but it was felt that there was need for more free seats. The new church was built on the opposite side of the road on land given by W. Postlethwaite, of The Oaks. This church was in every respect a departure from the simple country church, and was built to accommodate 479 people (104 free), at a cost of £1,678. The seats were allotted in

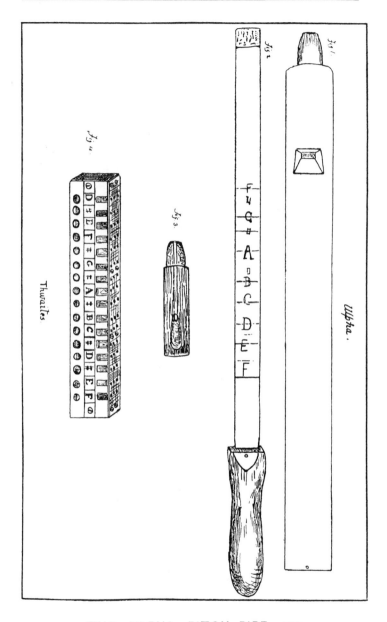

THE ULPHA PITCH-PIPE AND
THWAITES HARMONICON.

proportion to the subscriptions of the owners and the surplus sold by auction in the vestry previous to the day of consecration, June 11, 1854.

The de Thwaites were lords of the manor at an early date ; about 1280 William de Thwaytis, grandson of William, the first known lord, gave 1 acre of land to Furness, this is the field called Summer-ridding, behind the Punchbowl Inn, the small spring in the field is the Steward's Well mentioned in the deed. The de Thwaites family left the district at an early date for Ewanrigg ; part of their manor house still remains. The district passed into the hands of the Lowthers prior to 1697.

The old Pound, or Pinfold, of the parish is at Strands and is now in ruins. George Wilkinson was the last " pincher " ; the fine for impounding was 1/- for each animal and damages, if any.

At Ladyhall is the " Roman Road," an old packhorse track leading from the Duddon ford to Gornal Ground. In a small sheltered corner by its side is an oval, slightly excavated and crossed by a stream ; it is surrounded by boulders, rude walling, and slabs set on edge. This little amphitheatre was a halt for packhorse travellers, and perhaps a smithy as well.

Two cases brought before Mr. Justice Thompson, of Thornflatt, in 1657, show that Thwaites was not a law-abiding district :

" April 20, 1657. Hugh Hodgean, of Whitesham, against Edmond Myers, George Canny, and Thomas Taylour of Thwaites, for the breaking of his house, and taking £20 in moneys and other goods forth of the same."

" July 15, 1657. Anthony Fox and Ralfe Kitchen of Millom, Joseph . . . complained that the said persons did at Thwaites, within his Constablewick, rioatously assault and beat him with staffes, pitchforks, and other weapons, against the peace of his highness the Lord Protector, and is bound in £20 to prosecute his said information at the next sessions."

IV.—THE CASTLE.

MILLOM Castle stands in a position where lines of approach were limited and observation upon them easily maintained, the most important of the Duddon fords touched the Cumberland shore near a small hillock upon which an eighteenth century stone indicates that here the Lords of Millom exercised Jura Regalia. The road from the ford continued past the Castle to join " The Street." The Holme upon which the Castle stands comprised about 12 acres and is surrounded by low land, which in earlier days was a peaty morass of some 200 acres ; the two lower parts were crossed by stepping-stones to Low House and to Gallowbank, removed about 1850 and 1774 respectively. The Castle is not isolated, but forms a link in the chain of tower houses and castles which came into existence soon after Bruce's raids in 1316 and 1322, such as Muncaster, Irton, Piel, and Gleaston.

The main entrance to the Castle is reached after passing between a pair of fine seventeenth century gate-posts. The steps to the east door are fairly modern and give access to a ruined entrance tower, about 10 feet square with walls 5 feet thick. A door in the opposite wall opens on the court-yard, which is 33 feet by 27½ feet. The north wall of the yard is formed by the kitchen, and near the west end are the remains of the jamb of a portcullised doorway (E on plan), beyond this a gateway leads to the hall, 44 feet by 33 feet. In the 6-foot thick north wall are two large pointed windows with window seats, the eastern being 2½ feet higher, indicating the raised floor of the lord's dais.

Two doorways with pointed arches and chamfered edges enter the kitchen, which measures 30 feet by 21 feet. This room has two lights in the north wall, the hearth and oven are in the east wall and are provided with a central

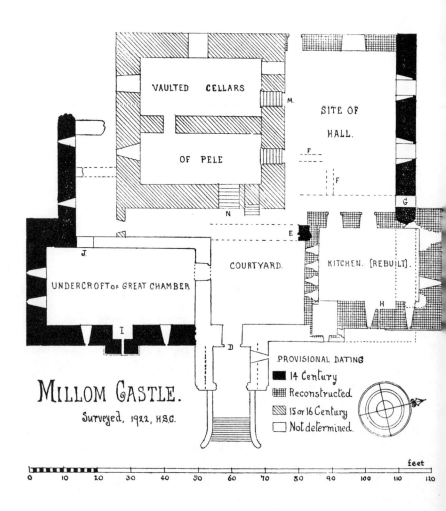

VAULTED   CELLARS

OF PELE

M.

SITE OF

HALL.

F

F

G

J.

UNDERCROFT OF GREAT CHAMBER

COURTYARD.

E

KITCHEN. [REBUILT].

H

N

I

D

MILLOM CASTLE.

Surveyed, 1922, H.S.C.

PROVISIONAL DATING

■ 14 Century
▦ Reconstructed
▨ 15 or 16 Century
☐ Not determined.

feet

0   10   20   30   40   50   60   70   80   90   100   110   120

THE HUDLESTON ARMS IN THE CASTLE COURT-ROOM.

Gules, fretty argent. *Crest, two arms holding a bleeding scalp.*

smoke hole (H on plan) ; the room above has a small mural chamber, 10 feet by 7½ feet. The kitchen wing is later than the hall or else has been reconstructed.

South of the courtyard is a large and important building with two floors, 43½ feet by 22 in extent. The ground floor is lighted by four splayed loops ; in the east wall is a fireplace (I on plan) from which a smoke hole led straight through the wall, which is here strengthened to compensate for the weakening caused by the fireplace. Beside the door into the courtyard another can be traced leading into the corridor on the west. This room was low and dark, yet entered by an ornate door, but there is no evidence of a staircase leading to the important room above ; indeed, there is no trace of a staircase in the Castle save in the Tower ; access to upper rooms must, it seems, have been by wooden stairs through a trap-door or externally to doors in the wall. The large room on the second floor must have been one of the features of the Castle, it contained a fireplace immediately above the one below but is provided with a chimney ; it had two doors, one in the east wall near the gateway tower, where a mural passage led to a chapel, in which a piscina has been found. At the opposite corner in the south wall a narrow door about 20 inches wide with an ogee head leads by another mural passage to a tiny chamber and thence to the corridor buildings behind. This room has not the characteristics of a hall and there appears no difference in date between it and the ruined hall ; it was evidently, therefore, for domestic use and may be regarded as the Great Chamber of Millom Castle.

The Pele Tower is about 50 feet square and has walls 7 feet thick, built of rubble with freestone dressings of a much later date than the rest of the remains, and is now the inhabited part of the Castle. It consists of a base-ment comprising two vaults, four floors, and a roof for-merly embattled.

The first floor was entered by a door from the east, 6 feet in width, and next to the modern door. There are three rooms, the largest was the kitchen, the others the

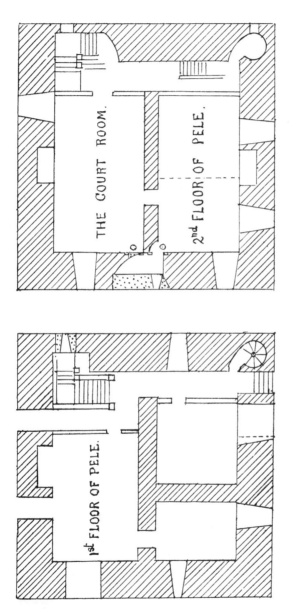

THE COURT ROOM.

2nd FLOOR OF PELE.

1st FLOOR OF PELE.

MILLOM CASTLE.—THE PELE TOWER.

buttery and a vestibule from which a narrow newel stair led to the second floor, the handsome oak staircase being built in the seventeenth century.

The second floor contained the Court-room, which measured 35 feet by $17\frac{1}{2}$ feet before the introduction of the oak stair reduced its dimensions. Before its use for the manor court it must have been the hall when the Tower was inhabited as a complete dwelling. It contains a square freestone fireplace above which is a medieval bracket rudely carved with a face, and above this the finely carved sandstone shield with the Hudleston arms with mantling, esquire's helmet, crest and motto, " Soli Deo Honor et Gloria," a beautiful piece of seventeenth century work. The small doors (O, O on plan) and the mural passage seem to be earlier means of communication between the rooms than the door in the central wall.

The third floor is divided into bedrooms but contains some fine old panelling; the next contains attics, from which it is possible to reach the parapet. The top of the tower is much the same to-day as shown in Buck's view, 1739, save that the ruined battlements must have been replaced by a horizontal parapet about 44 feet above the level of the moat, which can still be traced on the south and west sides and through the farm buildings on the north. This moat is the dyke by which John de Hudleston was empowered to enclose his house in 1335. There are traces of buildings and earthworks south-east of the Church and a ditch in the fields to the S.E. which includes the Church, though this is probably of very early origin.

The historical aspect of the work is difficult to treat, owing to the changes and the present ruinous condition, but after Sir John had obtained his licence to crenellate and enclose with a ditch it is probable that he and his son laid down the main lines of the work, the hall, kitchen, entrance tower, and the great chamber, which were only fortified by being within a curtain wall and surrounded by a ditch; there may have been an earlier and smaller tower than the present one. The Castle seems to have been largely destroyed about 1460, during the Wars of the

Roses. During the period of prosperity in the sixteenth century the Pele Tower was built and the semi-ruinous hall finally abandoned.

V.—INDUSTRIES.

THE land was wooded and consequently a place of woodland industries. Charcoal burning had already begun in the thirteenth century and by the time of Henry VIII most of the large timber had been felled. Here and there by the side of unfailing streams and gills are heaps of slag, the remnants of the old furnaces, where small charges of ore, brought by packhorse, were heated for several hours over charcoal until they became more or less reduced and could be forged into bars of iron. A date is difficult to fix, but iron smelting had been going on since Norman times. In the seventeenth century a larger type of furnace came into use. William Hudleston's will mentions his furnace at Ulpha, and Denton, writing in 1688, says that within thirty years £4,000's worth of timber has been cut down for the iron forges; another writer of the time includes a ship made from the timber, but says of the forges that Ferdinand Hudleston "was little or nothing profited thereby." In 1688 Ferdinand wrote to Sir Daniel Fleming, saying that his friends thought an eighth too high for the working of the mines and proposing a tenth. Running through Ghyll Scaur is Furnace Beck and beside it are remains of slag heaps. Iron ore of moderate quality was worked near Millom Vicarage and some was brought from Furness. In the early eighteenth century the Backbarrow Company mined at Millom, but not extensively; in 1718 several hundred tons of ore were taken from the " Oar Pitts at Millham," for which a royalty of a shilling in the pound was paid to Ferdinand Hudleston. The timber and other necessaries were brought from Conishead Bank ; the attempt was soon abandoned, though in 1777 it is recorded of Millom, " Here are Iron Mines."

The most interesting and best preserved of the early smelting furnaces is at Duddon Bridge, established in 1737. The earliest reference is in a letter from Sir Joseph Pennington's steward, dated 20/2/1736, " A scheme is on foot for erecting a Furnace at Duddon Bridge by Mr. Hall and Company," and a fortnight later he adds that work has begun, " And it's Reckoned to be one of the most beneficial works of ye Sort in England." This Cunsey furnace passed through many hands until it became the property of Harrison Ainslie and Company in 1828; they worked it until 1867, when it was allowed to fall into ruin. During its 130 years no changes were made, the charges were carried up steps to the top and the open blowing cylinders of 1785 with their primitive driving apparatus were still in place at the end. A sad entry in the Thwaites register records the burning to death of a little girl at the furnace. Iron ore was brought up the Duddon in flat-bottomed boats from Dalton.

Other industries were turning at Ulpha, but when bobbins became cheaper elsewhere the business died out; slate pencil making at Arnaby and at Hallthwaites, at the latter place was also a blacking mill assessed at £1 in 1840. The woollen mills at Thwaites are said to date back to the sixteenth century, the weaving shed being added in the seventeenth, and combing mills in the eighteenth. Whitehall, Whicham, was at one time a sickle factory. Ruddle was made until quite recently at Water Blean and " fairy pipes " are still found in the old workings in Crina Field.

At Kirksanton, prior to 1798, 140 acres in 23 fields were let out to villagers for the cultivation of hemp for the rope walk, which is said to have been on the Green; it was worked by hand in dailes or strips locally called Tenter Runs.

Fishing is recorded at an early date, for there is an indenture of 1338 between the monks of Furness and John de Hudleston regarding a fishery at Houbergh, which appears to have been Borwick Rails. Tithe fish were paid to the Vicar of Millom as Rector of Chapel Sucken within

DUDDON BRIDGE FURNACE, ABOUT 1880.

the last century, and this payment was stated to confer certain rights on the owners of fishing boats. The port of Millom was not of great importance until the opening of the Hodbarrow Mines in 1855, and the Ironworks in 1869; indeed, when the railway was made there was no Millom station, but Holburn, the population of Millom Above and Millom Below being then only 980. In 1566 the Commissioners for the Superintendence of Ports reported that at Powesfoote, that is Crook Pool, Borwick Rails, the deputies were Ralph Latus, Thomas and John Fox, and Thomas Dickenson. The report concludes, " There is no Towne ne Inhabitations nere Scituat the same but Howses much dispersed one frome another alongst the Sea Coaste, of the Inheritance of Anthony Hudleston Esquier. There hath none heretofore used to give license for the Loding or unloding there. There is no Shippes, Vessells ne any maryners." About a century ago " Burrow Crails " harbour exported corn, slate, wood-hoops and rods for coal baskets and imported coal.

Reference has been made to the unsuccessful attempt to mine copper in Ulpha; in connection with this it is interesting to note a letter (9/6/1771) from John Cooper, of Wha House, to Sir James Lowther:

" Sir, In your Manor of Thwaites there has lately been discovered an Ore, supposed to be copper, but of which no Trial can be made till your Consent for that purpose is obtained. I once hinted my Desire to treat with you about the sd. Royalties in the sd. Manor, and should be glad to know your terms immediately; and hope, if any Application has, or shall be made to you concerning them, you will not enter into any Contract without giving me a fair Chance. Mrs. Cooper joins in Complts. to Sr. Jas. & Lady Mary, with Sr. yr. much obliged

and very Hble Servt.

Jn° Cooper.

P.S. Yr. immediate ansr. will be a particular favour, and if you wou'd chuse to have any Trials made, I shall be happy in executing yr. Commands."

John Cooper was the oldest brother of the Rev. Dr.
Myles Cooper. He inherited the Whahouse (now Duddon
Hall) estate, but was forced by financial difficulties to sell
it in 1784. For many years prior to his death in 1778 in
France he was a Major in the Cumberland Militia.

VI.—OF MANY THINGS.

THE CLERGY.

THE first Rector of whom we have record is Adam
(c. 1160), he was probably succeeded by " Benedict
de Millom," who appears in certain charters. To the published lists of the Vicars of Millom can now be added five
new names. John de Ypres came in 1369, on the death of
William de Sutton, and left in 1372 to go to Bootle. John
de Ypres' place was taken by Henry del Hay. Richard
Scharppe died in 1430, and Adam de Erghome, jun., took
his place, to be followed in 1464 by George Yveson. In
the 1495 Inq. p.m. Myls Hudylston is recorded as vicar,
he belonged to the Whittington branch of the family, and
in 1464 claimed direct descent from Sir Richard, Lord of
Millom in 1330.

There does not appear to have been any break at
Millom during the Commonwealth; Bootle gives a better
picture of these troublous times, for Samuel Dodding,
M.A., was sequestered from the parish, as the following
document, dated 1646, shows:

" It is ordered yt upon Certificate from ye Comtee
of Parliament for ye County of Cumberland yt ye
Rectory of Bootle is sequestrated (wch ye sd Comtee
are hereby desired to make) this Comittee will take
care for settlinge of a godly and able minister in his
stead."

Thomas Millington, B.A., who followed the short in-
cumbency of William Greene, was also sequestrated, his
petition for restoration to the living in 1660, although
piteous in its pleading, was not successful.

" To the Right Hoble the House of Lordes Now
Sitting in Parliament The humble peticon of T. M.
Rector of the parrish Churche of Bootle in the County
of Cumberland in the Diocese of Chester Most Humbly
showeth That yor peticoner haveing beene legally possessed of the Rectory aforesaid hath beene Sequestred
and eiected for many yeares to the utter ingrie of him-
selfe, his poore wife and Children only for praying for
his Matie in publique as in duty he ought to doe.

" Therefore yor Peticoner prayeth yor Lordships
to take compassion upon yor Peticoner's sad condition
And to grant forth yor Lops order that yor Peticoner
may for his present maintenee receave and enjoy the
Fifths of all profitts Ariseing from the said Rectory
and that the other ffower partes of the said Leving may
be despose of into the hands of the Church Wardens
and overseers of the poore of the said parrish upon
Accompt untill the Intruder be Eicted by Law . . ."

Richard Hutton may have been the Intruder ; he was
certainly at Bootle in 1665. In 1672 he sought to obtain
the living of Aldingham and wrote to his " friend and
kinsman," Sir Joseph Williamson, urging him " to be
pleased to cast an auspicious eye upon me to improve yor
interest on my behalf to the Right honourable the Earle
of Arlington. . . ." A week later he gives reasons for
leaving Bootle. Aldington, he says, is a no more considerable place than Bootle, " only yt I have been forced for
some years by gone, not onely to preach but fight against
Sacrileg, the Patron of the place invading the Church's
patrimony and instid of patron will needs becom Impro-
priator ; So yt I have much exhausted much of my estate
in defending the Church's right (wich by the blessing of
God and Justice of the Reverend Judge I have hitherto
done maugre all Sacreligious harpies) So yt being vexed

into Lawsuits, I should take it as a happiness to spend
the remainder of my time in the service of God and my
venerable mother the Church of England in peace; and
should look upon yt more obscure rurall Cure as a
Patmos . . ."

The following letter from the Vicar of Corney,
William Benson, B.A., written in 1692, throws light upon
the manners of the time. It is addressed to " Mr. Josiah
Lambert att his office in Kendall " :

" Sir, These 2 lines may certify yu yt we have in
our parish one John Pirt & his wife Isabell yt are
Comon Sabbath-breakers they bake ther bread upon
the Lords day as will Appear by the evidence of one
Richard Jackson in Corney who was an eye witness
to yt action Isabell the wife of the above named Pirt
did bring forth her full born Son within 20 weeks after
the were married, we did in yor Court at Ravenglass
present one Wm. Jackson for not receiveing the sacrament of the lords supper & pirt did advise him to
come to you & Mr. Trotter & Inform you concerning
all the defamation yt ever were heard agst me & you
would sett him att liberty & he should be free. I pray
you be not slow to punish this man who is admitted
of all his neighbours for impiety you may by a citation
(if you please) wch you may send by this bearer call
him at Kendall the next Court, he is a man of noe
courage but rich enough therefor cause him to pay
for his Roguery the bearer will confirm what I averr
If you enquire of him; wt I have here writte I pray
you doe not discover for if he knew he would scarce
faile to do my cattell a mischief this is all from him

who is

Sr yr humble Servt

Wm. Benson.

THREE NOTABLE CLERGYMEN.

The **Rev. John Postlethwayt,** M.A., (1650-1713) was
the son of Matthew Postlethwaite, of Bankside. After
passing through the Whicham and Millom Grammar
School he entered Merton College. Later he became
head of St. Martin's School, London, he was promoted
to the Deanery of York, and in 1697 became head-master
of St. Paul's School; among his testimonials for that
position being one from Richard Bentley. He is buried
at St. Austin's Church, London; his funeral sermon,
preached by John Hancock, D.D., is printed under the
title of *The Christian Schoolmaster.* Postlethwayt contri-
buted £256 towards the purchase of a glebe farm at
Fawcett Bank, Cautley, for Millom Parish Church.

The **Rev. Myles Cooper,** M.A., D.C.L., LL.D., son of
William and Elizabeth Cooper, of Wha House, now
Duddon Hall, was born in 1737. He was educated at
Carlisle Grammar School under the Rev. Miles Wenning-
ton, of Greystone House, Thwaites, and at Queen's
College, Oxford. After being usher at Tonbridge School
he returned as Chaplain to his college. The Governors
of King's College, New York, were seeking a man capable
of becoming Vice-President, and eventually of succeeding
Dr. Samuel Johnson as President. On the advice of Dr.
Bentham, Cooper was selected and sailed in 1762. He
was appointed Professor of Moral Philosophy and a
Fellow of the college; the following year Johnson retired
and Cooper became President.

Under his vigorous and aggressive policy the College
grew in size, wealth, and prestige; a medical school was
started, New York's first public art collection, assembled
in the College library, grants of land secured, and New
York Hospital founded, with Cooper as a chartered
member. In 1771 he visited England as an embassy of
the American Church and of his College requesting the
appointment of Bishops for America, support for a plan
for educating and Christianising the Indians and for the
grant of a charter to change the College into a great

American University endowed by the King. On his return the sky was clouded by revolution, and he spent the next two years supporting the Loyalists, becoming the most hated of them all. After Lexington he had to flee for safety to a British warship in the harbour, and a few days later managed to escape the wrath of a mob, fleeing in his night clothes to a friend's house. He returned to England in 1775 and reassumed his Fellowship, and for a time was curate of Paddington, a position which he resigned in favour of his Loyalist and fellow Cumbrian friend, the Rev. Jonathan Boucher.

His English career was just as stormy; his Fast-day sermon in 1776, *National Humiliation and Repentance Recommended,* led to so much controversy that the Bishop of London was asked to withdraw his support, and Walpole tried to make an example of him before Parliament. In 1777 Cooper began his ministry of the Episcopal Chapel in Cowgate, Edinburgh; he died in 1785 and lies buried in the old Restabrig cemetery of that city.

The **Rev. Miles Wennington,** M.A. (1726-71) was born at Greystone House, Thwaites, and married Elizabeth Cooper, of Wha House. He was elected headmaster of Carlisle Grammar School in 1750 and eight years later ordained, nominated to be a Minor Canon of, and licensed to preach in, the Cathedral. He became Vicar of Bootle and died there. His will gives a picture of the funeral customs of the time, with the mutes in deep black, with hat-bands, and with scarves reaching to their knees, often actually weeping, owing to their tipsy condition.

In the Name of God, Amen.

I, Miles Wennington late of the City of Carlisle, but now of Bootle in the County of Cumberland, Clerk, do make this my last Will and Testament in Manner and Form following: In the first Place, it is my will that my Funeral be conducted in the plainest and most frugal Manner. It is my Will, that there be no general Invitation, nor any Invitation at all except

of a few of my own parishioners, not exceeding a
dozen at the most, with whom I was known to be the
most intimately connected in my Life Time, and that
these be entertained with Bread, and Cheese, and
Ale. It is my further Will, that there be no Distribution of Hatbands, Scarves, Hoods, and Gloves,
except to my two Trustees hereafter mentioned, to
whom I order Silk Hatbands and Gloves. It is my
Will, that my Body be carried to the Grave by six of
the poorest men of the Parish of Bootle, to whom I
order double their ordinary Day's Wages, and Bread
and Cheese and Ale for that Service. It is my further
Will, that there be no promiscuous Distribution of
Money at my Funeral commonly called a Dole or
Dale, a custom of which I have always disapproved,
but that, instead of such Distribution, there be, as
soon as may conveniently be done after my Decease,
a Distribution of five Pounds among such poor House-
holders or others of the Parish of Bootle, as receive
no Allowance from the Parish; this Distribution to
be at the Discretion of my Trustees . . . .

And lastly, it is my Will, that my Coffin be of the
plainest and most unornamented Kind, such as are
used for the poorest people; and that there be no
Funeral Sermon. So much for what concerns this
wretched Body."

HUNTING

Millom Park is but a remnant of a larger park, remains
of which are scattered about South Cumberland; when
John de Hudleston allowed the monks of Furness to
enclose their pastures at Butterilket, about 1285, he stipu-
lated that the fences should be low enough to allow the
deer and hinds to leap over them. Around the Castle are
several fields, known to-day as " Sewals," a sewel, in
hunting parlance, was a line of feathers fastened on twine
a foot or two above the ground, in order, says Turber-

ville, in 1573, " to amaze a Deare and to make him refuse
to passe wher they are hanged up." Deer Leap Well,
near Low House, may also be a reference, for a deer-leap
was a low place in a park-pale which allowed deer to
enter the park from outside ; the privilege of having deer-
leaps was granted only by the king.

Poaching, of course, was frequent ; the last tenant of
Hall End is said to have been hanged at Gallows Bank
for poaching in Ulpha Park.   There is an interesting reference to some Thwaites poachers in 1552, when Edward,
Earl of Derby, complains to the Captain of the Kynges
Maiesties garde and Chancellor of the Duchy of Lancaster, the Rt. Hon. Sir John Gates, " that where he is
seized in his demesne of fee or feetail of a certain park,
called Broughton Park, with divers franchises and liberties
thereto belonging ; and where by divers estatutes of the
realm no man shall haunt unlawfully Jeffray Benson of
Thwattes yeoman, Gawen Ascought Jeffrey Postilthwatt
and Gilbert Symons of the said town and county yeomen,
and John Ascogh and Nicholas Dixon of the same, hus-
bandmen and divers other evil disposed persons to plaintiff
unknown arrayed after the manor of war with daggers,
bows, and arrows, long pykid staves, swords, buckellars
and other unlawful weapons assembled at a certain place
in the said park called Hangman's Oke on June 12
(Trinity Sunday) last past and there not only riotously pur-
sued, chased and hunted with greyhounds deer but also
killed and carried away 3 tegges (does in their second year)
to the pernicious example of others if not punished." He
therefore prayed for a writ of Privy Seal against them.

There is an interesting letter, dated 1657, from Col.
Kirkby, who was a companion in arms of Sir William
Hudleston during the Civil War, to his nephew, Daniel
Fleming.   " I have had some descourse with your cousin
Kirkby concerning the ' intended progress of hunting ' of
the Cumberland gallants.   When you go to Naworth you
may tell them that Sir William Hudleston's absence need
not hinder this hunting at Millom.   Your cousin Kirkby
who has command of the game in Sir William's absence

will show them all sport for the killing of a brace of bucks, and give them such accommodation as his little house will afford."

Towards the end of the eighteenth century the Earl of Lonsdale enquired into the profit and loss account of the Millom deer. They strayed out of bounds, often staying out all night, lying amongst the corn; in winter they had to be supplied with hay or they died, and as there were over a hundred the grass was cropped so short that pasture had to be found elsewhere for cattle; in addition, two keepers had to be employed. The herd was sold to a Darlington man at £1 per head. Nets and dogs proved no use in rounding them up, shooting was ineffectual, since it became increasingly difficult to approach them, snares for their feet and ropes for their antlers failed; at last five men noted for their marksmanship set themselves the voluntary task of shooting the remainder; after weeks of patient effort only two remained, then but one, an old stag, who for a long time defied all stratagems, until hounds were collected and it was forced to break bounds; several fine runs followed before it was finally killed.

THE ENCLOSURE OF THE COMMONS.

The eighteenth century enclosure movement was, considered as a whole, disastrous to the poor of England and produced social troubles which, even to-day, are still unremedied. In certain forms it had advantages, and to this class belongs the Enclosure Bill of 1820, affecting the waste lands of Millom. These "Waste Lands," or "Commons," were situated at Poole House Bank and the Marsh "called Arnaby Marsh otherwise Millom Marsh," and were 1,500 acres in extent. The Earl of Lonsdale was owner of these lands and "all Mines or Minerals within and under the Commons"; he, with the Rev. John Myers, the Rev. Philip Kitchin, and divers other persons, were entitled to right of common and, after the passing of the Act, specific parts were alloted to the owners again.

After the passing of the Bill, even before the actual enclosure took place, it became illegal for " any person or persons whomsoever to cut, dig, grave, pare, subvert, take or carry away any Turves, Flacks or sods or any part of the Land, Soil, Earth or surface in, upon, of or from the said commons " or to " make or burn any mound or mounds of Earth or Soil, or to mix any Earth or Soil with Lime."

The more important part of the Act relates to the reclamation of Arnaby Moss from the Duddon or the sea by which " it was liable to be overflowed or inundated " ; it rendered it lawful for the Commissioners " to make such mounds or embankments in Millom along the strand of the Duddon and the sea as their discretion and judgement may determine necessary." The cost of this embankment was, however, to be met from the rents of the tenants of the adjoining lands. The Embankment was made in 1830 at a cost of £3000, and reclaimed 250 acres of land.

THE QUAKERS.

In 1653 George Fox wrote in his Journal, " Now there were great threatenings given forth in Cumberland that if ever I came there again they would take away my life. When I heard it I was drawn to go into Cumberland, and went to Miles Wennington's, in the same parish from which these threatenings came, but they had not power to touch me."

John Wennington (1597-1662) was probably Registrar of Millom, he gave £30 to the poor dwellinge between Loggan Becke and Scalehooke," his sons were Myles, of Ashes, and William, of Greystone House : in those days probably one estate. Fox stayed the night at Ash House, then went on to Bootle, where he had a very stormy time ; staying at Bootle-in-Millom. This was taken by Canon Rawnsley to mean Millom, but considering all the facts, some place in Bootle, perhaps Millholm, seems more probable. The Journal continues, " In the meantime some

of those called the gentry of the country had formed a
plot against me, and had given a little boy a rapier to do
a mischief with it.   They came with the boy to Joseph
Nicholson's house to seek me ; but the Lord had so
ordered it, that I was gone into the fields . . . not finding
me in the house, after a while they went away again, so I
walked up and down in the fields that night, and did not
go to bed as very often I used to do."   James Lancaster
(d. 1669) was of North Scale, Walney ; Fox had met with
a hostile reception there and on recovering consciousness
had found Lancaster trying to protect him from the stones
Mrs. Lancaster was throwing.   Lancaster travelled a
great deal with Fox, especially in North America, and was
one of the earliest Quaker missionaries to Ireland.   He
appears to have rented land in Millom from Joseph Nicholson, payment being made   through Sarah Fell, as her
Account Book shows :

" 1677.   ffeb : 25 To mo Recd of Ja. Lancaster more
in pt of 10 li 10s due to Jos. Nickolsons order in
London being his rent of Land in Millan for 1 yeare.
004. 04. 00."

Joseph Nicholson and his wife were among those who
suffered in the New England persecutions.   In 1661 he
was imprisoned in Dover Castle, and in 1658 he is mentioned in the Calendar of State Papers, when William
Thomson, of Thornflatt, a Cumberland J.P., sent to the
Keeper of Carlisle Goal " with all constables of Muncaster the Bodyes of Richard Robinson and Joseph
Nicholson lat of Boutel who are to keep in your said Goale
till the next Quarter Sessions of the peace to be holden
for the said County . . . they have both been lawfully
convicted before me that they have wilfully and Malitiously
disturbed two publick Ministers of this Nation contrary
to the late Acts of Parlement in that case provided."
Their offences had been committed at Corney, Drigg, and
Muncaster.   It appears from a letter of the Keeper of
Carlisle to Mr. Secretary Scrobell that the term of
imprisonment was not long.

There is an entry in the Chester Register (1677-98) concerning two Friends from Stoneythwaite, Ulpha, " Johnem Tyson et Elizam ejus ux. Edwardson et Johnem Tyson, Quakers and for standing Exc." John and Elizabeth Tyson were buried in the Colthouse Ground. In the Ulpha Register appears an entry " And in dispute concerning Quakers 02. 01½."

The Quakers have passed from the life of South Cumberland leaving as their only memorial the tiny burial place on the Lancashire side of the Duddon at Ulpha. Tradition says that meetings were held at Woodend, where there is still a building called " Quakers' House," and that those buried in the Dunnerdale Sepulchre were from that place ; the last interment was in 1745. Efforts were vainly made to turn the place into an orchard and vegetable garden, until finally the daughter of the Vicar of Seathwaite planted the trees and shrubs which to-day shade the stone seats running round the inside of that enclosure not fifty feet square.

It is interesting to find a close friendship existing between the Fells, Quakers of Swarthmoor, and Captain Huddleston, of Barfield, Whitbeck. One entry in Sarah Fell's Account Book runs : " 1674. By mo given a man yt brought 2 Turkies ; 2 Capons and a pce of venison, from Capt. Huddlestone of Scogarthe barne to Bro. Lower, Mothers acct 000. 01. 00."

SCHOOLS AND CHARITIES.

In 1686 an enquiry made under the Commission of Charitable Uses found that some person unknown had given the parishes of Whicham and Millom £16 annually for a free Grammar School. A decree was made by the Commission ; Millom took exception to this and the case went to the Chancery Court. The school had been in existence in 1540, when the money was decreed to be paid annually from the Cumberland Crown Revenues. Millom claimed as founder a pre-Elizabethan monarch ; Whicham a servant of Elizabeth, Hodgeston. The case was heard before the Chancellor (1687-91) and referred to Chief Justice Wright of the Northern Circuit to enquire into the best position for the school and its best form of government. The schoolhouse, it was decided, was to be built at the Church gate, not in " Code Ellis," and an equal number of trustees were to be appointed from each parish ; all the trustees were dead in 1746, and it was agreed that the Lord and Lady of Millom with the Rector of Whicham be appointed perpetual trustees. There were many petty disputes about the school. In 1602 John Bylane, late schoolmaster, " finding himself unable to continue the Care and charge of the said School any longer and being willing to surrender it up for the good of the said parish to such a one as is able to discharge the said place sufficiently and to that end hath made choice of one Richard Bulfield to keep the said school as by his resignation " in 1598. The new schoolmaster, it seemed to the County Receiver, had not been officially appointed, therefore he refused to pay his salary, but later reversed his decision.

The Rev. William Wells, Vicar of Millom, was charged with taking the school revenues and not using them to the good of the parish ; in 1687 he said he had been master there 18 years and, though clearing himself of misusing the money, fresh arrangements regarding trustees were resolved upon. The schoolmaster was generally a young man about to enter holy orders ; the £16 was found to be too small, so in the latter part of the eighteenth century a small quarterage was introduced, afterwards raised to four or six shillings, with a higher rate for children outside the two parishes. There were, about 1840, some fifty or sixty scholars.

Mrs. Bridgett Huddleston, who died in 1714, followed the example of Joseph Hudleston and left £100 to found a school in Millom ; the money being lent on bond to a Mr. Law, who became insolvent about 1780, so that the bequest was lost.

In 1809 William Atkinson bequeathed to John Steel £800 to be invested in public funds ; £2 10/- was to be devoted to the giving of flour and oatmeal from the mill at Upper Beckstones to the poor. The remainder was divided into three portions : one for poor scholars of both sexes to be taught in Millom Above, either at School Ellis or at The Hill; the second for Millom Below, to be used as John Steel and his successors should think fit; the third for the poor of Thwaites, either at Thwaites School or any fit place. Not more than 4/- was to be paid for any one poor scholar, and not that if a scholar " could be taught well and diligently for less." From the foundation of the Hall Thwaites School until 1825 the incumbent of Thwaites also acted as schoolmaster, for both offices being deficient in remuneration, the emoluments of one supplemented the shortcomings of the other. The Rev. J. Ormandy was the last incumbent master. The Parish Schools were re-built in 1863 at a cost of £565, and in 1878 they were leased to the Millom School Board.

About 1840 Samuel Clemnson, of the Mill, distributed 46 shilling portions of meal and 2 two shilling portions. There were two schoolmasters at Thwaites then ; 8 children were taught at 4/- a quarter and 8 at 3/- ; Millom Below had one master with 16 pupils at 3/6 each ; and in Millom Above were three mistresses with 21 pupils paying 3/- each.

James Goad, of Gleaston, afterwards a scholar at Sedburgh and schoolmaster at Swarthmoor, went to a school, perhaps belonging to the Friends, at Arnaby. It was kept by Robert Russell, who boarded his pupil with his brother William at Roanlands. Goad stayed only 19 weeks before returning to his own school at Dendron. Mrs. Jenkinson (d. 1896, aged 78) used to talk of the school being kept by Ellen Wilkinson in a small building now used as a potato shed; her mother, born in 1789, also remem-bered the school at Arnaby.

Opposite Park Head is a cottage at one time well-known as a school, especially for its high standard of Latin. The last master was J. Jackson, of The Hill. The school grounds were bounded by Millom Park on one side, on the other was unenclosed common, since awarded to

Park Head farm and Dashet Gate. Near the former farm is the old cock pit, 26 feet in diameter and 9 inches deep. The contests here were famous and brought spectators from all over the district; as many as fifty pairs were often fought in one day. The scholars superintended the contests, a King and Queen were elected, the last known being John Kirby and Miss Hunter.

Miss Frances Esther Millers, of Duddon Grove, in 1843 erected and endowed a school at Buckman Brow, Thwaites, for the education of girls in domestic work, the endowment was increased to the Rev. George Millers. The school is now closed, but the funds are used to assist the girls of Thwaites and Broughton, by means of grants to obtain further education.

In 1809 the Rev. John Myers, of Dunningwell, established a school for the education of 20 girls, the daughters of " sober and industrious labourers of the parish," in what is now Green Reading Room.

The Charity Commission of the early nineteenth century found that much of the money left for charitable purposes had been diverted to other sources. At Millom the interest on £32 which had been formerly distributed to the poor, was paid to the man who " worked a hand organ at the church." The Rev. Robert Crompton left £5 to the poor of Whicham; there was also £16 6s. 4d., the origin of which was unknown; a large part of these sums had been devoted to " flagging and pewing the church." Ulpha was entitled to a share in a charitable bequest made by John Middleton, of Ulverston. The Commissioners, however, could find no trace of this money, but £17 10s. had been invested by the parish officers and the interest applied to the poor rate; when the Commissioners suggested the propriety of using this money for a charitable purpose, a vestry meeting decided to devote it to the buying and listribution of Bibles, Testaments, and religious books.